FLOWERS AND DREAMS

◆◆◆

A Coloring Book of Beautiful
Botanical Symmetry

©2015 C.L. Aldridge

Illustrations by: C. L. Aldridge

ISBN-13: 978-1543055139
ISBN-10: 1543055133
Second Edition

BONUS PAGES

From the Artists other books and shops

The Adult Coloring Book
Of Flower Inspirations

Flowers and Flyers

Flowers and Whimsy

PLUS "The Turtle"
CLAldridgeArt on Etsy
PDF and Digital
Downloads

Also by C. L. Aldridge

Adult Coloring Book of Flower Inspirations
Beautiful Floral Patterns, Botanical Mandalas,
Gemstones, Lovely Words and More!

- I love this artist and this book has everything I love about her work, and then some! You can't go wrong with Flower Inspirations! - June 7, 2016 ~ *Teresa Z*
- C. L. Aldridge has hit it out of the ballpark again! Just as with her first book, "Flowers and Dreams," this one is filled with the most unique and gorgeous floral coloring pages you'll find. Her pages are designed with consideration for any medium you choose to use. I'll be anxiously awaiting the release of a third book! - June 10, 2016 ~ *E. Siegel*

Flowers and Flyers
Adult Coloring Book of Flowers, Songbirds, Hummingbirds,
Butterflies, Owls, Ornamentals and More!

- I have all 3 of C L Aldridge's books. I own lots of adult coloring books. These 3 are at the top of my list! - Sept. 30, 2016 ~ *C. Ames*
- Beautiful and relaxing to color! This is my first C. L. Aldridge book, but it will not be my last. I love that the pictures are one-sided, so I don't have to worry about bleed-through. Sept. 30, 2016 ~ *L. Mason*

Travel Size Book of Flowers, Birds Butterflies and More!
Your Coloring Book for the Road.

- Measures 6" x 9", just the right size to tuck in a purse, a travel bag or a desk drawer.
- 36 (12 from each of the larger books above) perfectly sized 5" x 7" illustrations for the busy colorist on the run.
- Easy to remove pages to mount on greeting cards, in frames or just satisfy the creative urge to color something beautiful.
- Single-Sided pages. 60 lb medium weight paper.

Flowers and Whimsy
Ornamental Floral Patterns, Butterflies & Dragonflies...

- This book is absolutely beautiful. If you are a C.L. Aldridge fan, you have to add this to your collection. Dec. 12, 2016 ~ *Cheryl C.*
- With her accomplished style and artistry, this is a great gift for a fellow lover of coloring, or someone who has her other books and would enjoy more. Dec. 12, 2016 ~ *Jill B.*

For all the colorists across the world that
have shared their talent with me and encouraged
me to keep drawing each and every day.
Thank You!

And a very special thank you to colorists Virginia Sanders Cole
(front cover), Susan Curry, Lisa Johnson and Karen Oderkirk
(back cover), for so generously allowing me to use their colored
renderings of my drawings on the cover of this book.
Also, a big shout out to Susan Curry for her wonderful
additions of background foliage to "The Turtle" bonus page!

IMPORTANT INFORMATION FOR USING THIS BOOK

- This book contains 24 hand-drawn illustrations, SINGLE SIDED (back is blank)

- Each illustration is printed in TWO SIZES, a full size page and a crafters size (suitable for a 5" x 7" frame, mounting to a greeting card face or scrapbook page, etc). Please note the crafters sizes are also single sided and are printed two on a page.

- The pages are printed on #60 lb bright white paper which performs well for all brands of colored pencils and crayons, without the need of a blotter page.

- To avoid any "Uh Oh's" and the associated disappointment, **Marker and Gel Pen users are STRONGLY ENCOURAGED to USE A BLOTTER SHEET** behind the drawing to avoid any possibility of bleed through to the next page. Several blank blotter and color testing pages are provided at the end of this book.

- Most IMPORTANT of all: Relax, have fun, stand-up and stretch often, and remember that sometimes the most beautiful things come from what we think at first are mistakes, but which turn out to be art's way of working magic!

This Book Belongs To:

_____

_____

© 2015 C. L. ALDRIDGE

©2017
C. L. ALDRIDGE

©2015 C. L. ALDRIDGE

© 2015 C. L. ALDRIDGE

© 2015 C. L. ALDRIDGE

© 2015 C. L. ALDRIDGE

© 2015 C. L. ALDRIDGE

© 2015 C. L. ALDRIDGE

© 2015 C. L. ALDRIDGE

© 2015 C. L. ALDRIDGE

© 2015 C. L. ALDRIDGE

© 2015 C. L. ALDRIDGE

Flowers always

© 2017 C. L. ALDRIDGE

make me happy!

© 2015 C. L. ALDRIDGE

Flowers are

Fundamental

© 2015 C. L. ALDRIDGE

© 2015 C. L. ALDRIDGE

© 2015 C. L. ALDRIDGE

C.L.Aldridge ©2015

© 2015 C. L. ALDRIDGE

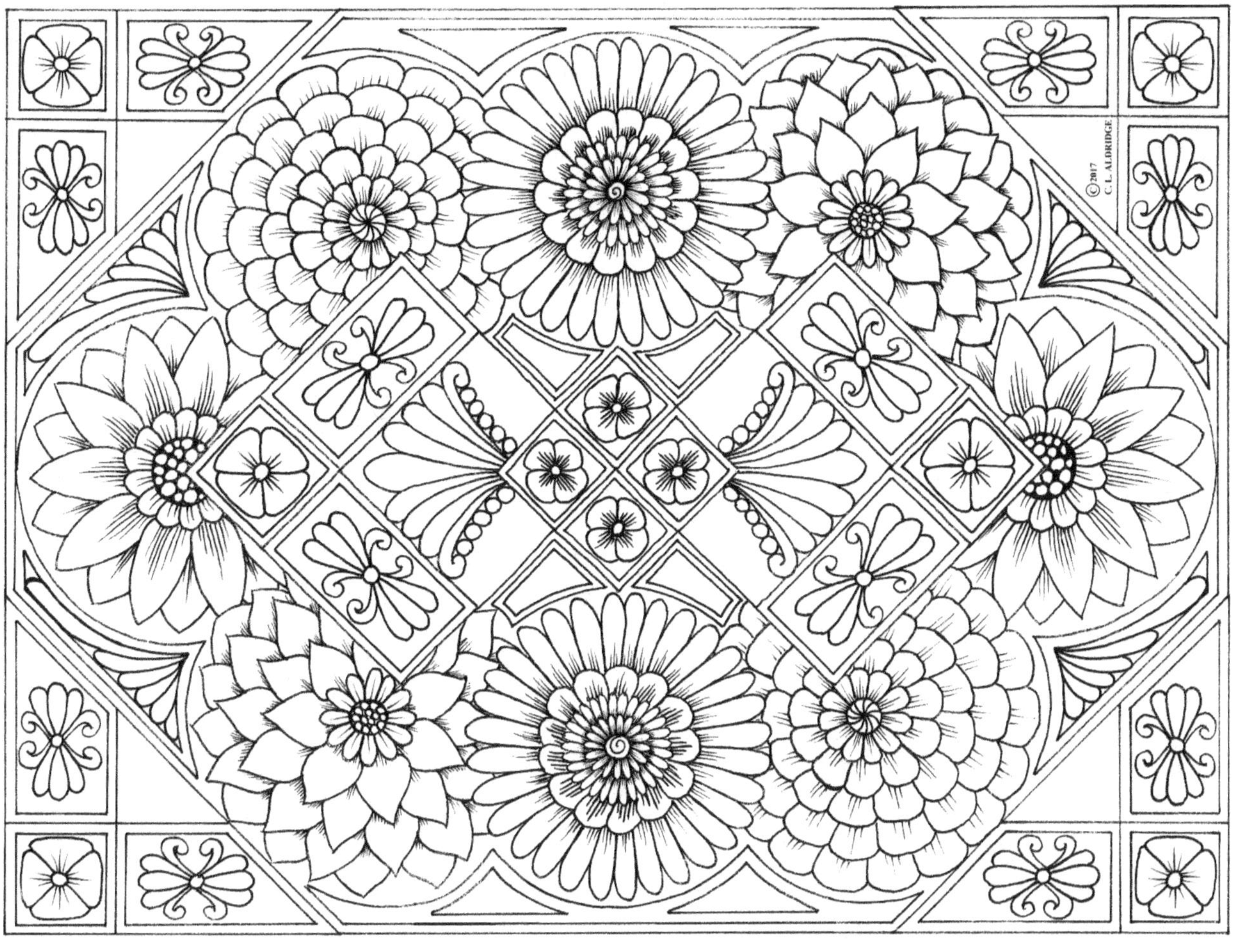
© 2017
C. L. ALDRIDGE

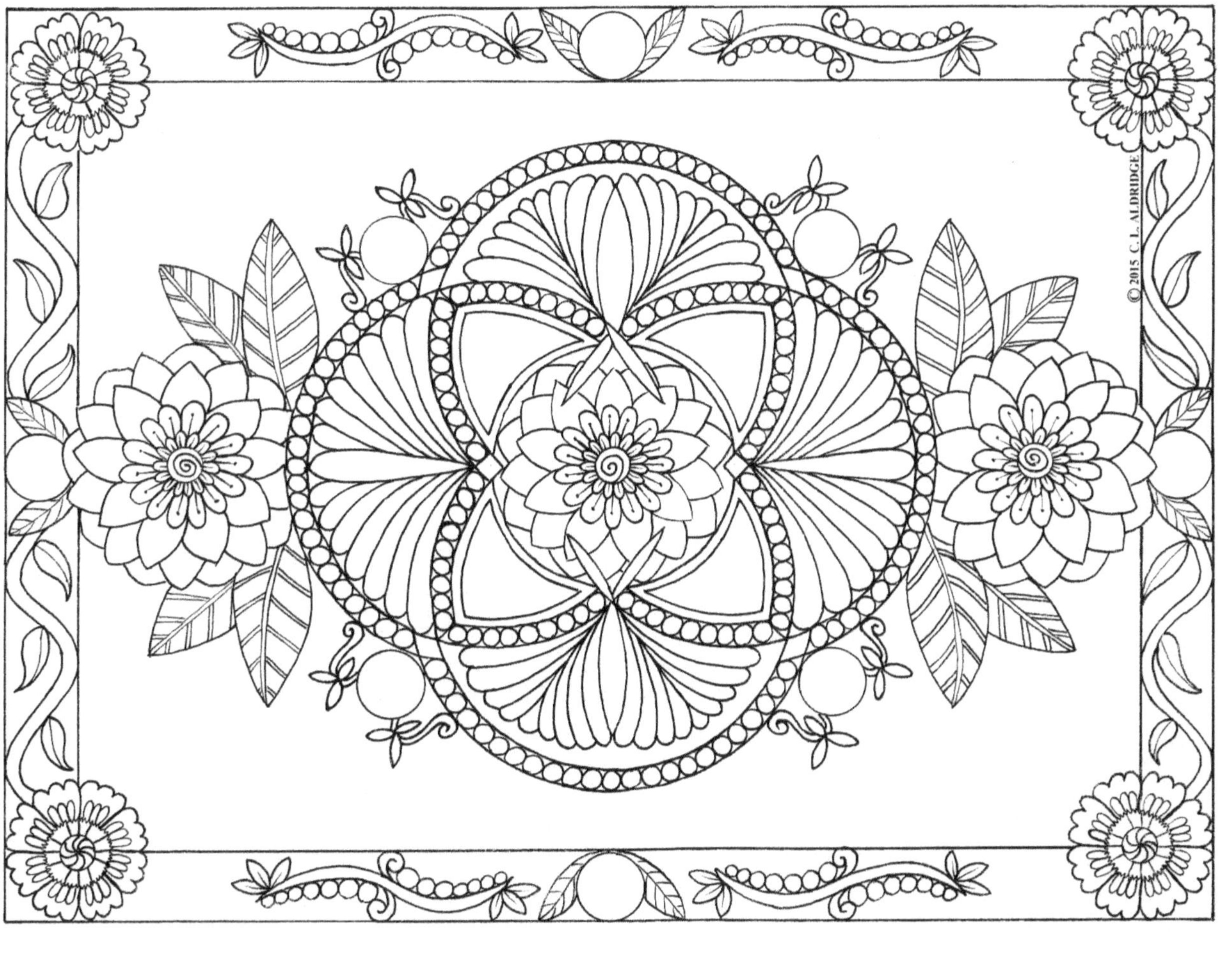
© 2015 C. L. ALDRIDGE

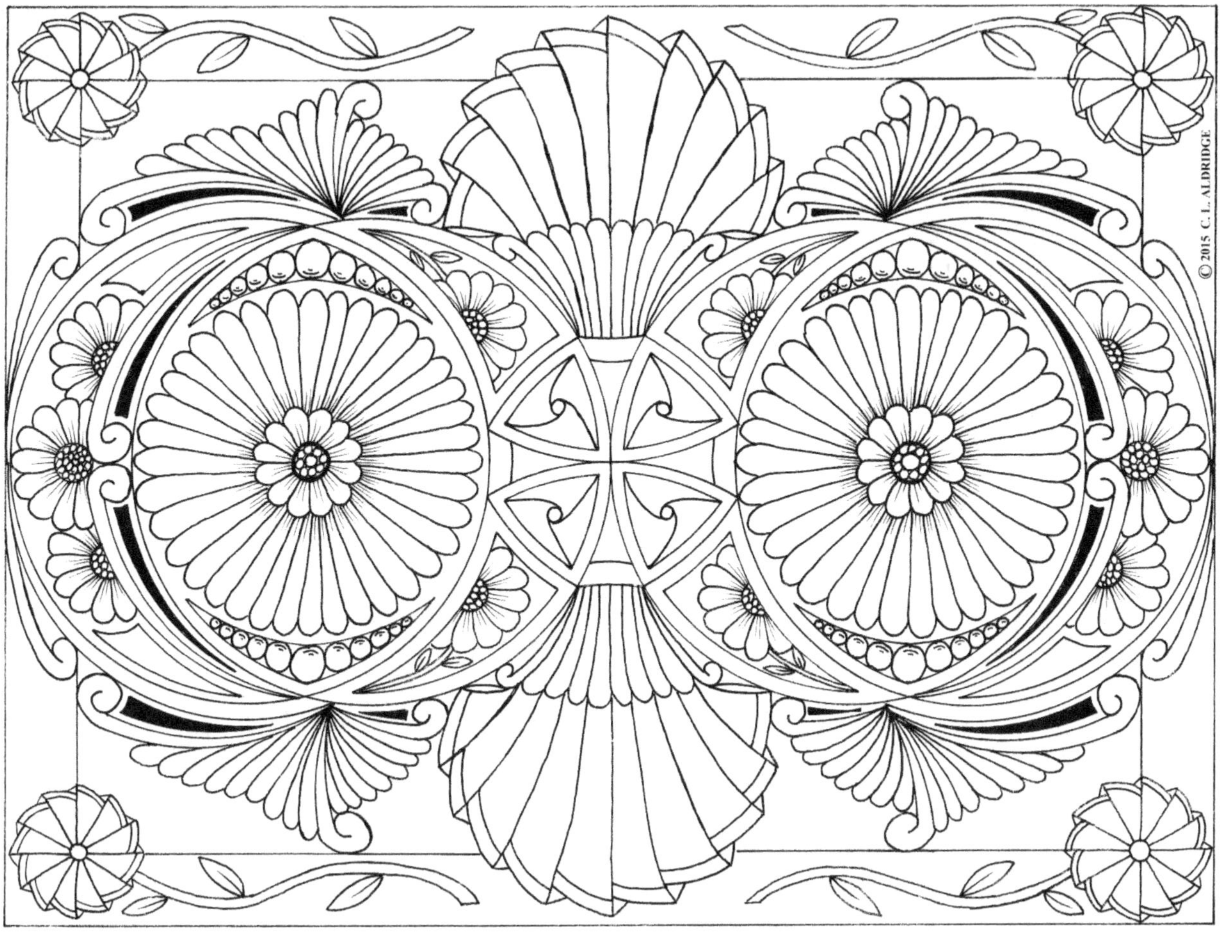
© 2015 C.L. ALDRIDGE

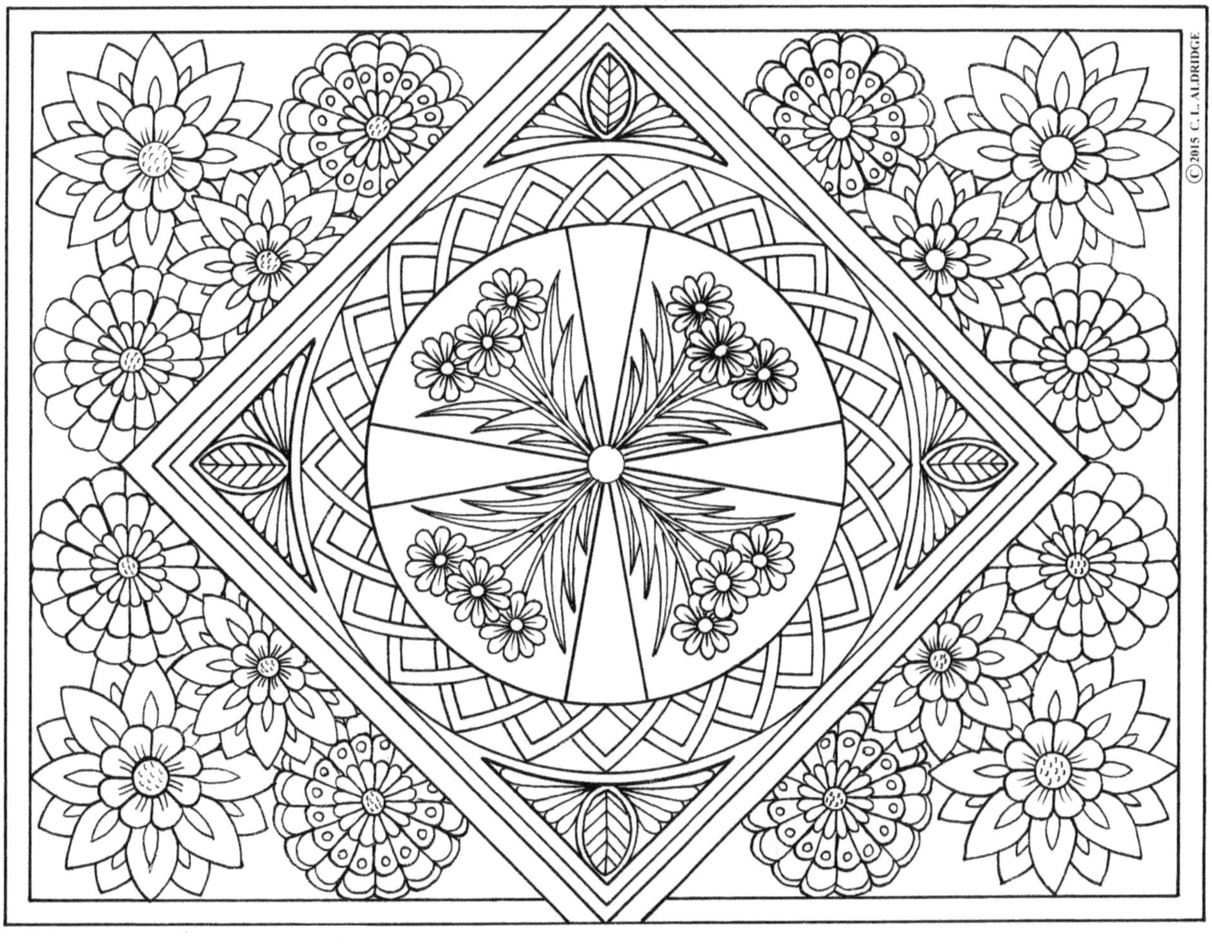
© 2015 C.L. ALDRIDGE

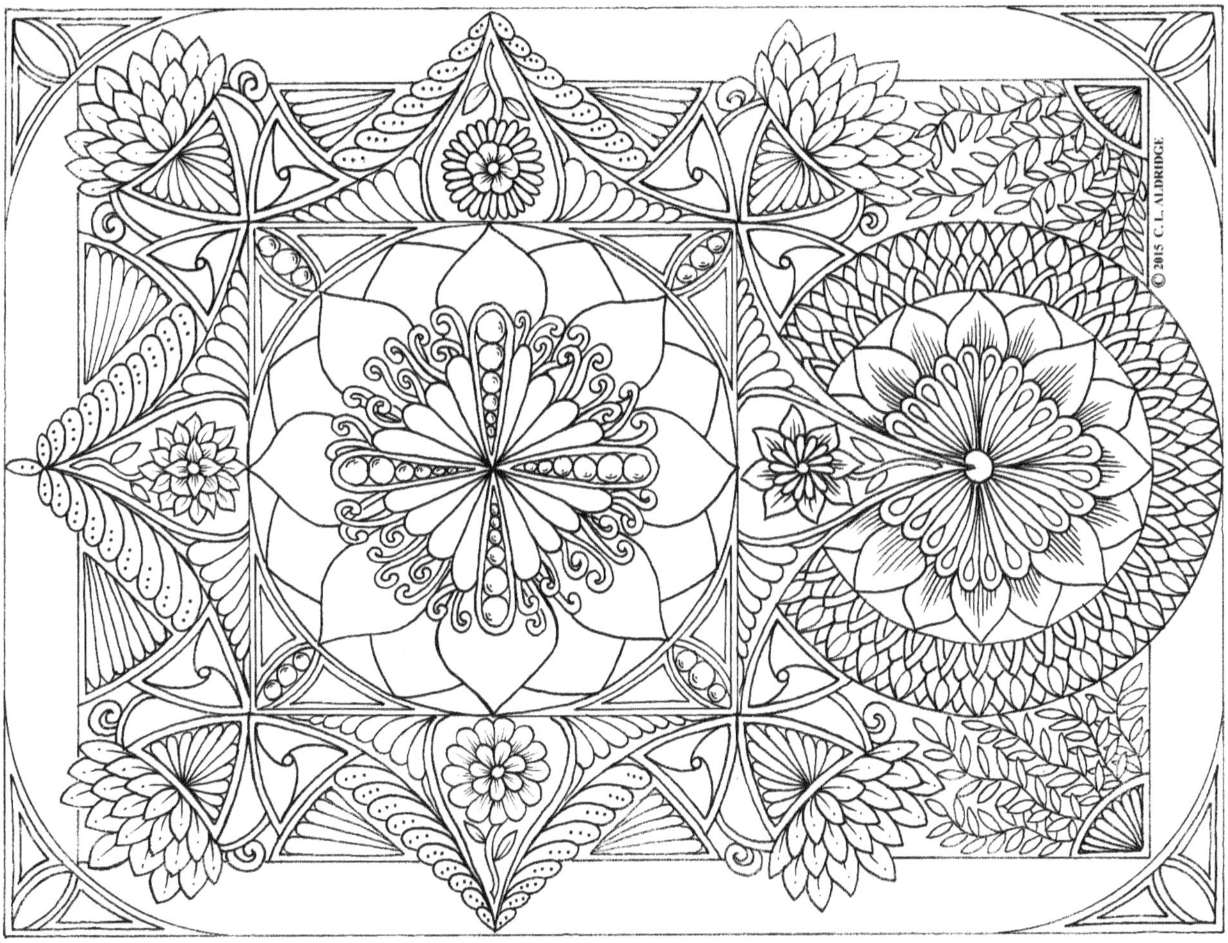
© 2015 C. L. ALDRIDGE

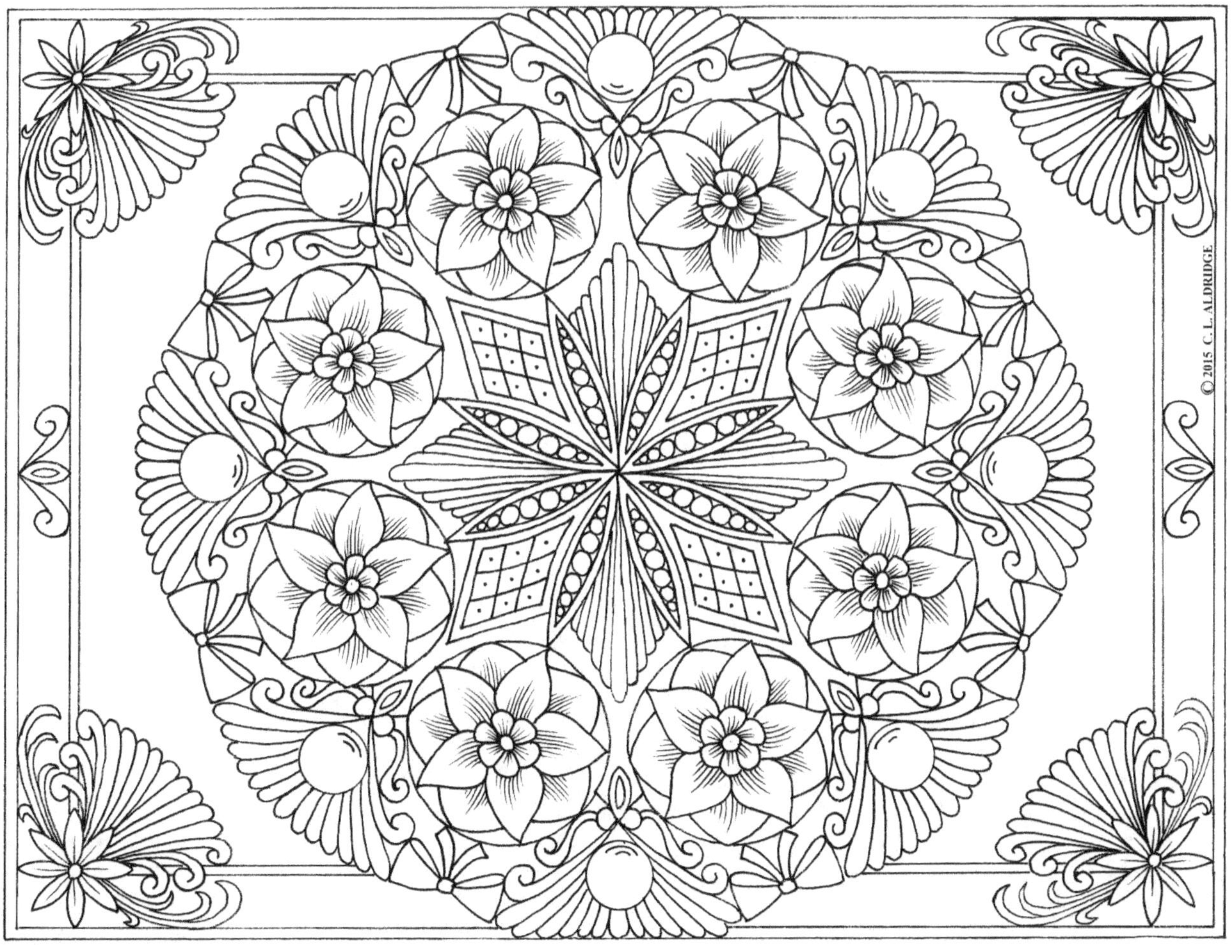
© 2015 C. L. ALDRIDGE

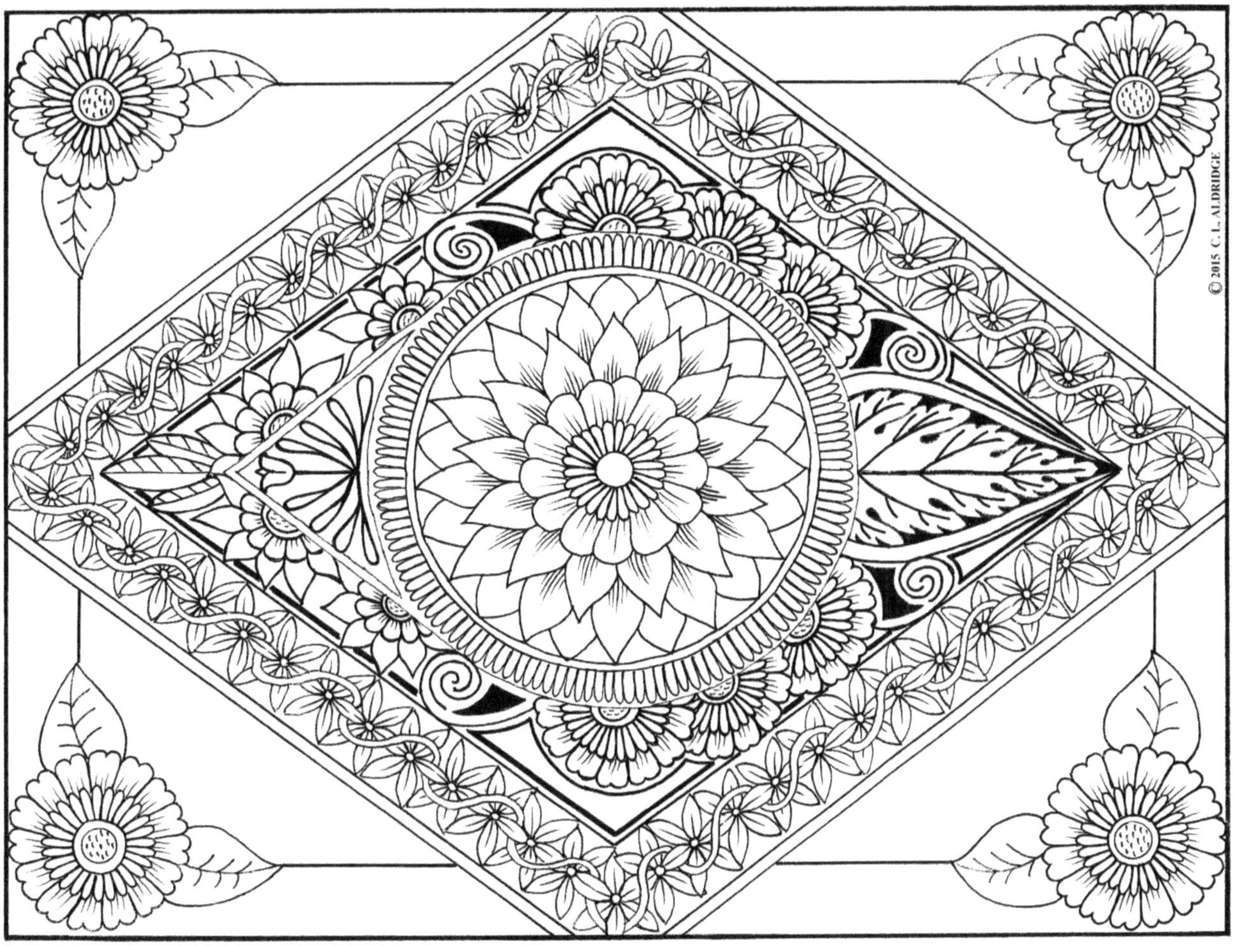
© 2015 C. L. ALDRIDGE

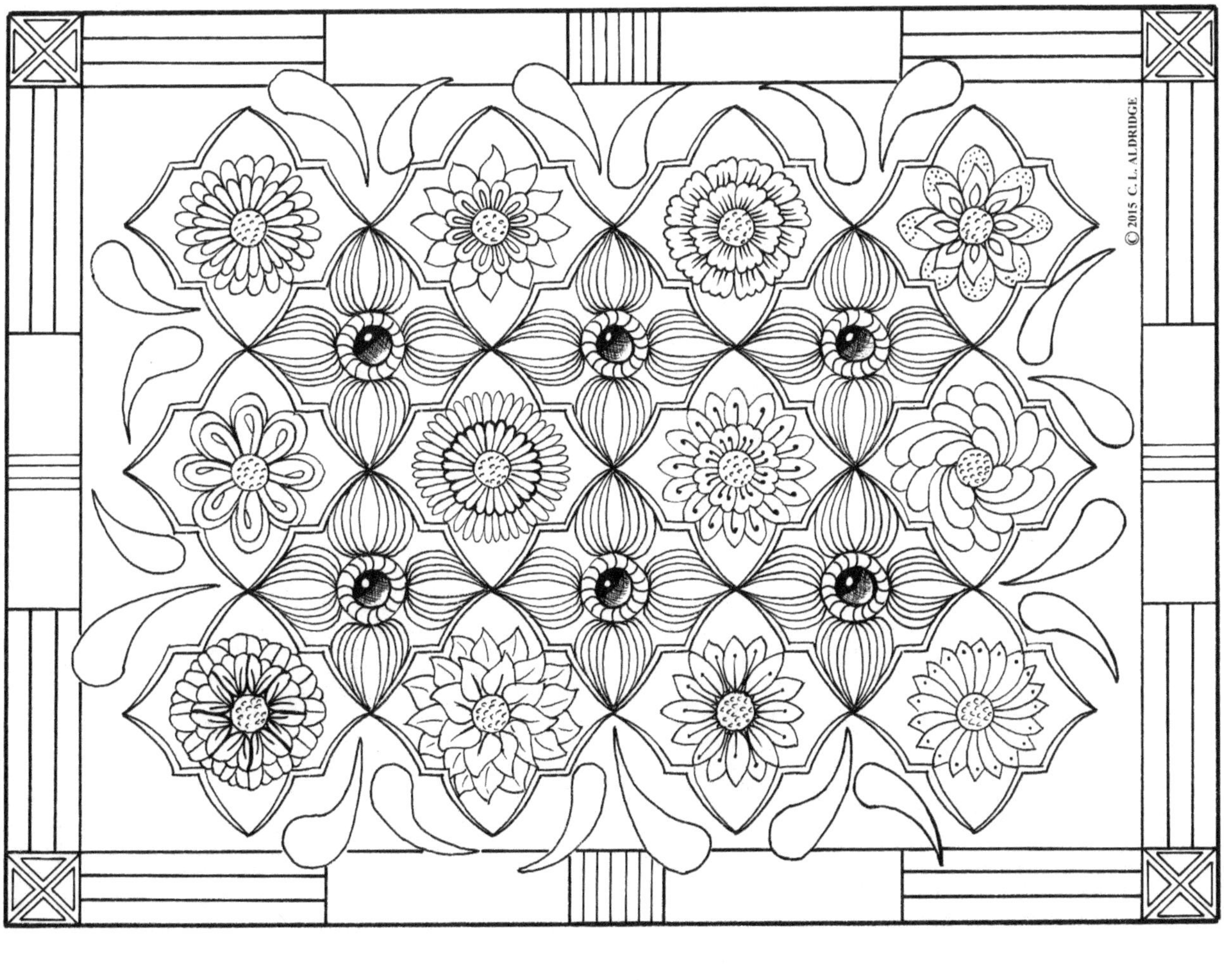
© 2015 C. L. ALDRIDGE

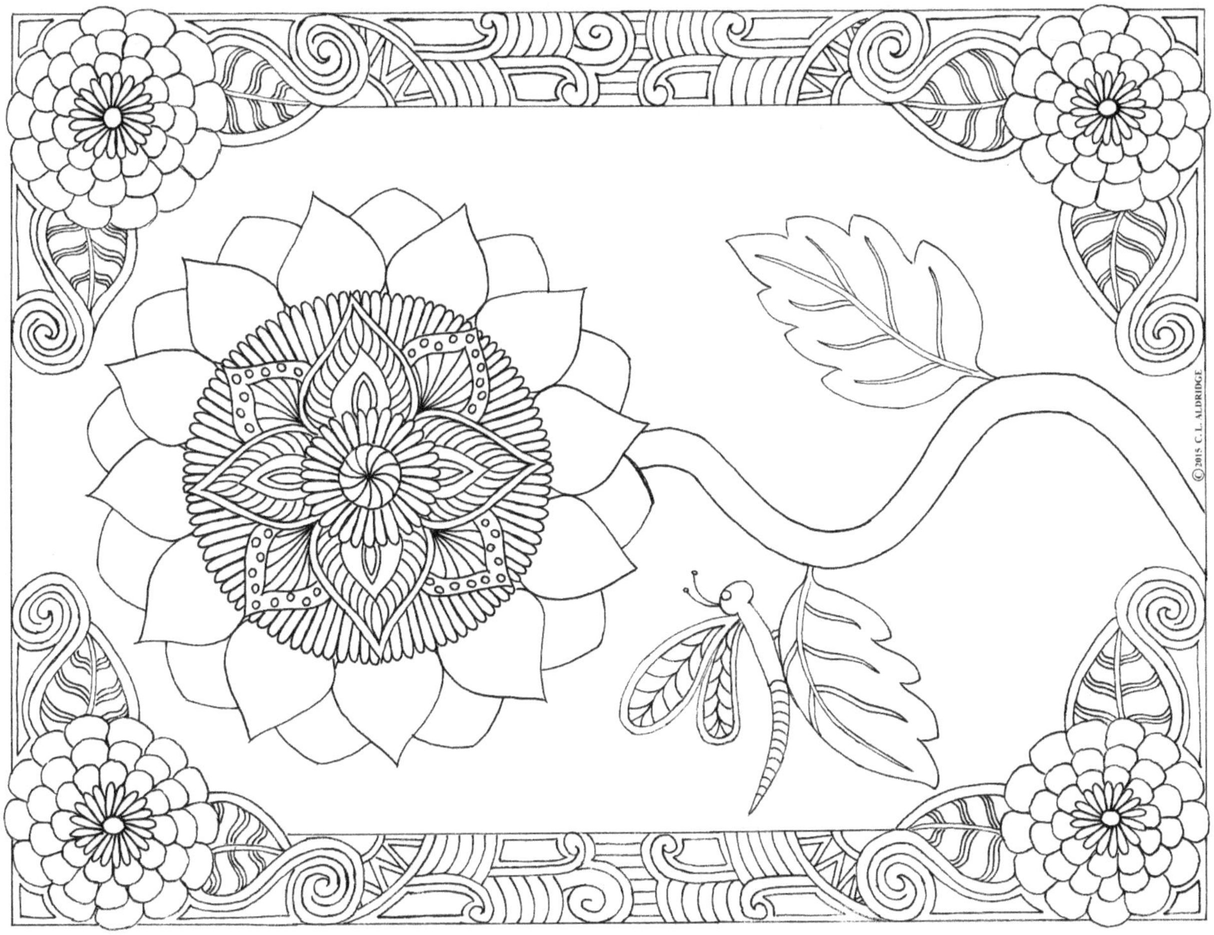
© 2015 C. L. ALDRIDGE

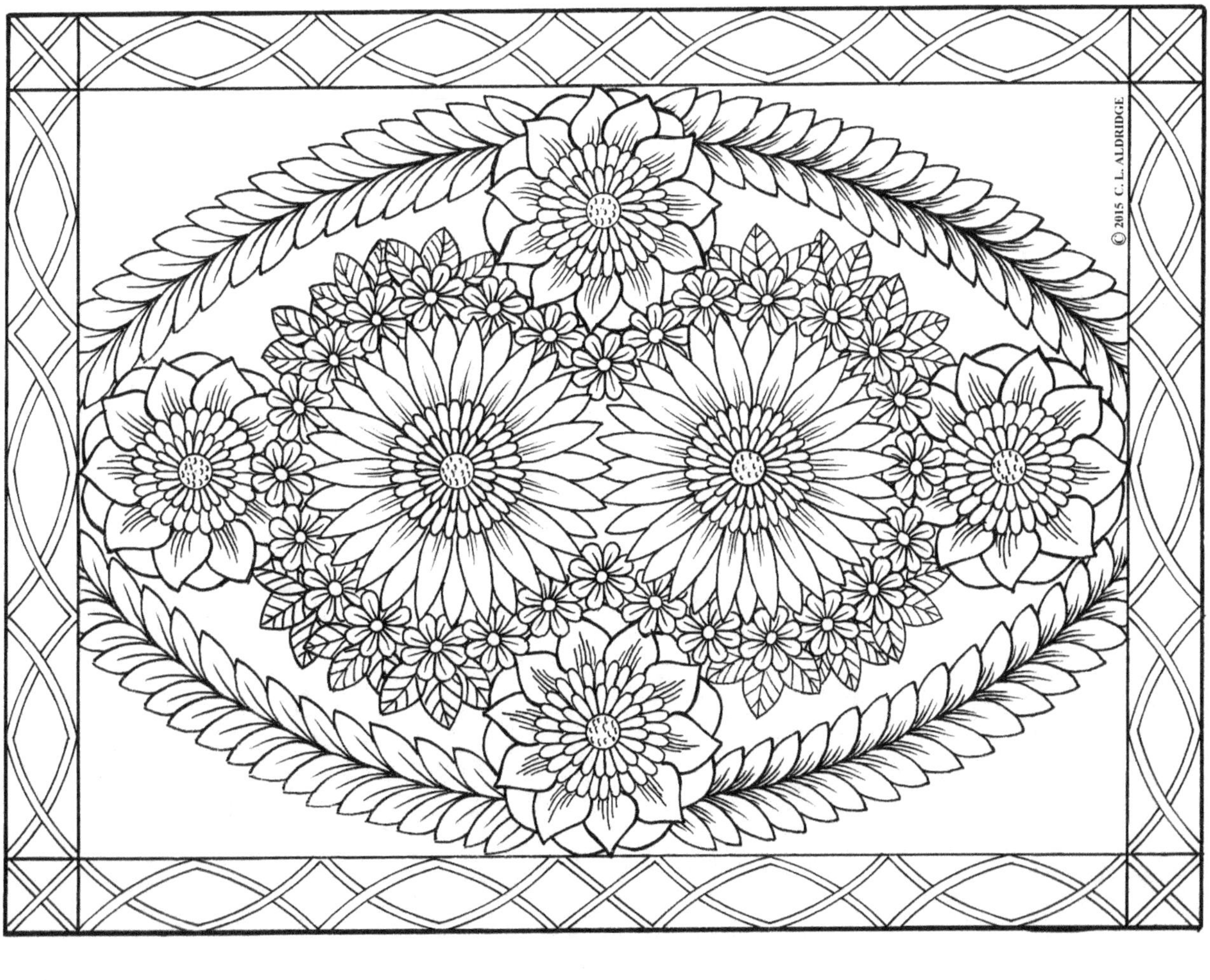
© 2015 C. L. ALDRIDGE

© 2015 C. L. ALDRIDGE

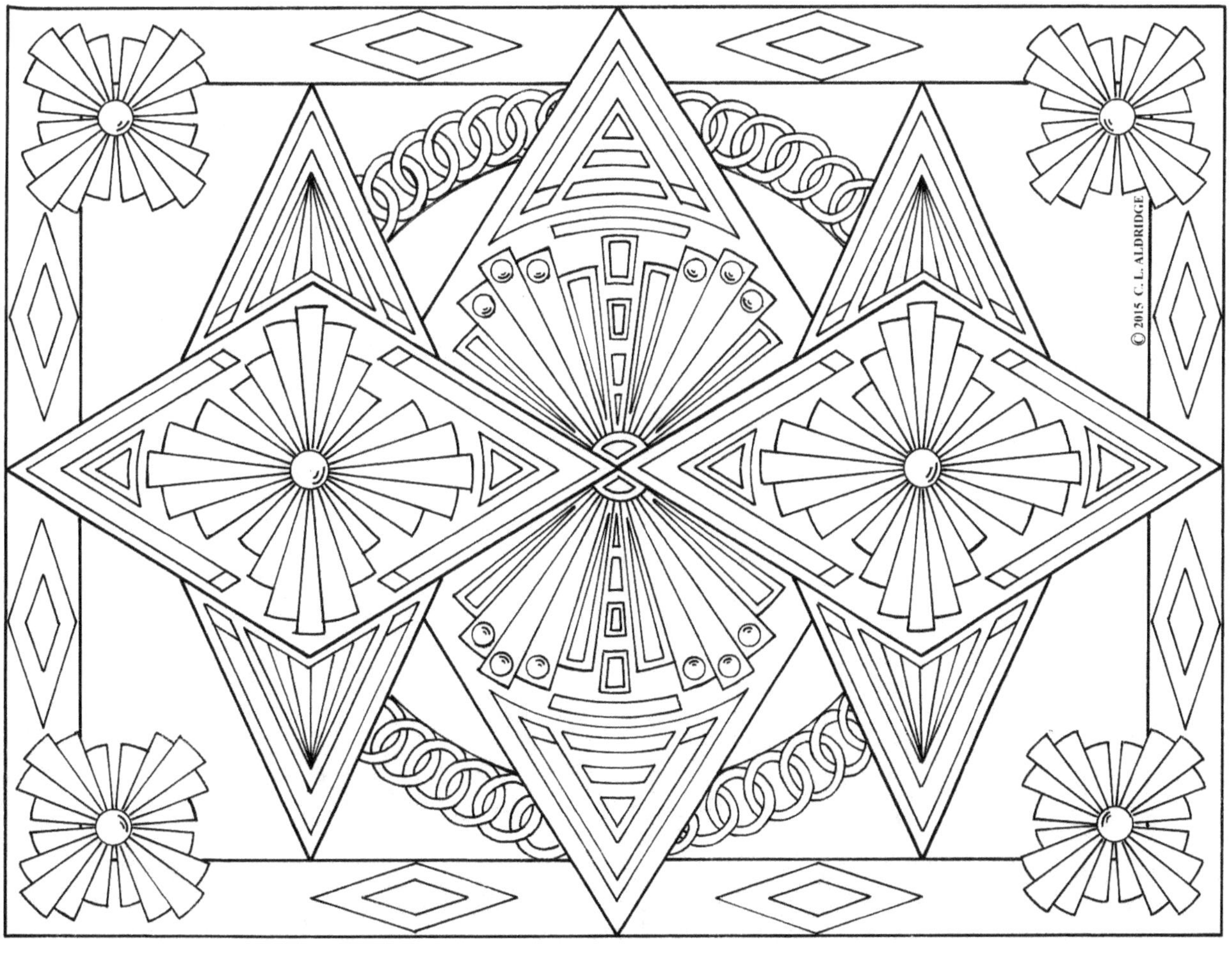
© 2015 C. L. ALDRIDGE

Flowers always

make me happy!

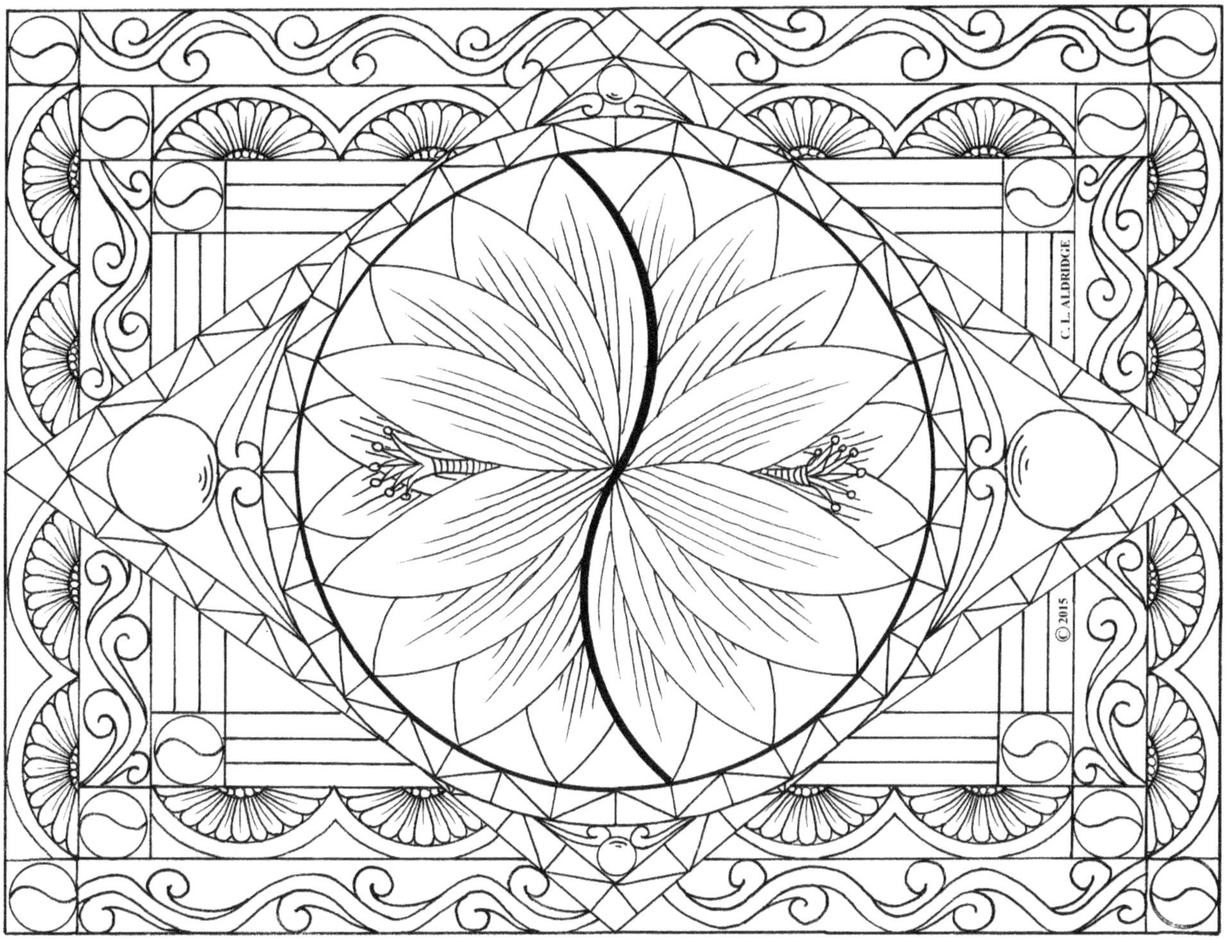
C. L. ALDRIDGE
© 2015

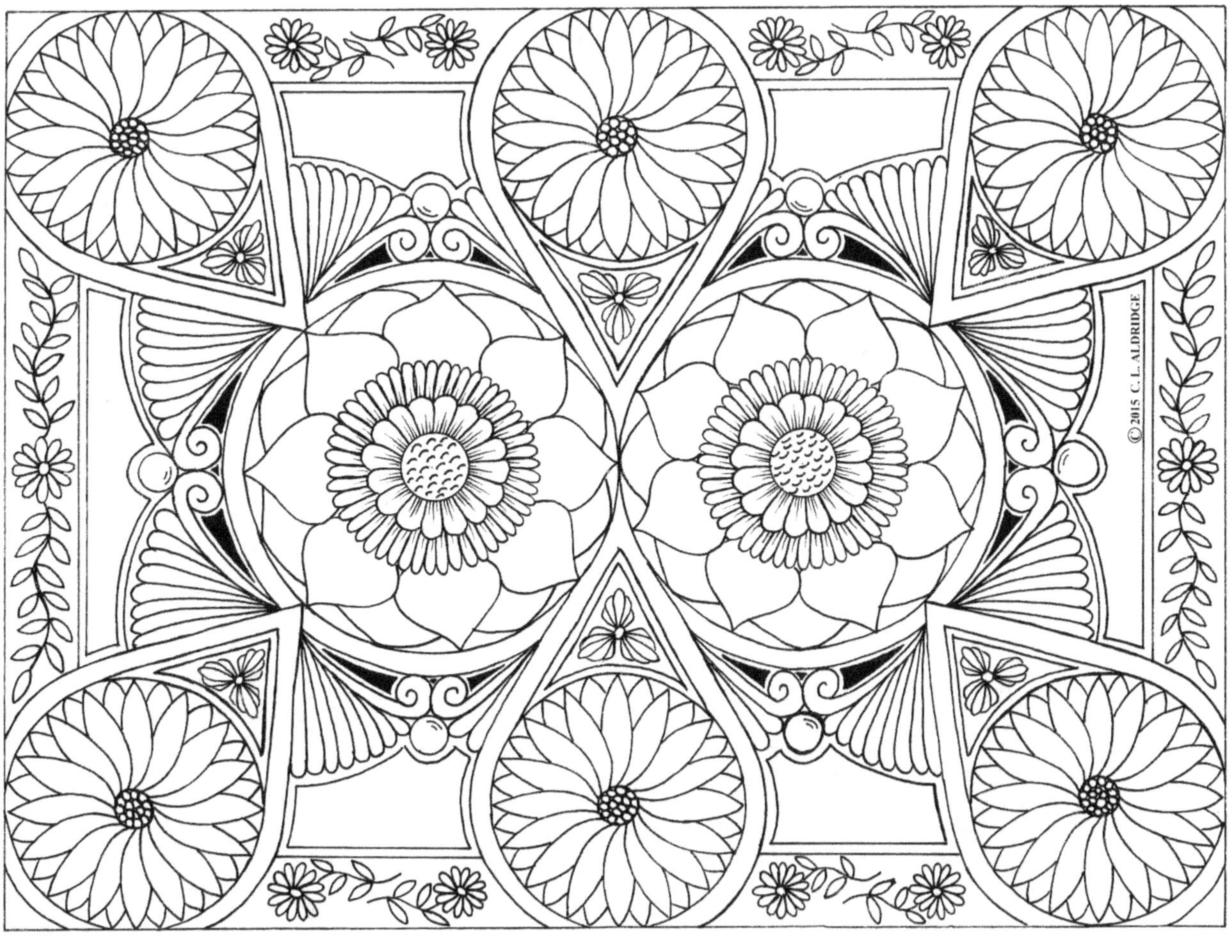
© 2015 C. L. ALDRIDGE

Flowers are

Fundamental

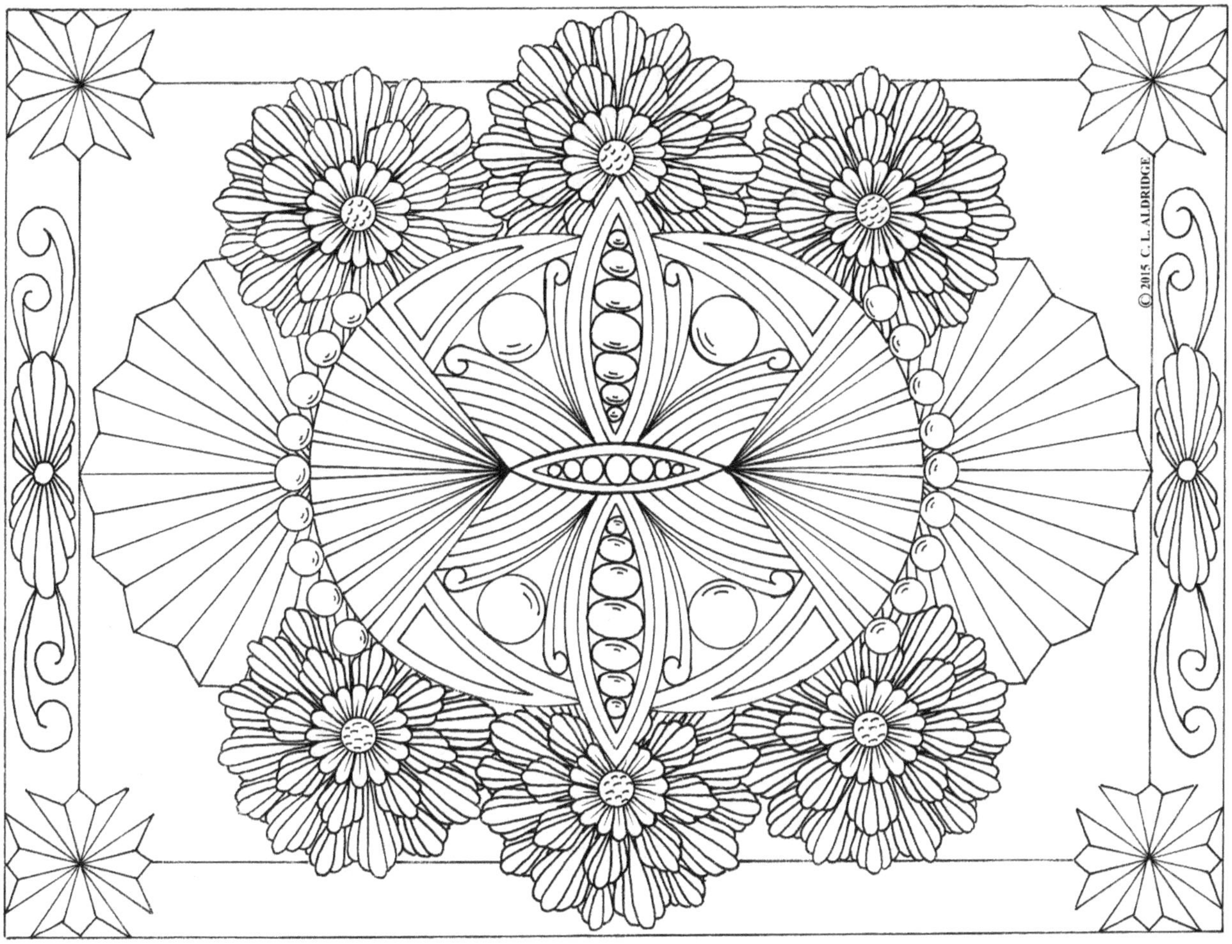
© 2015 C. L. ALDRIDGE

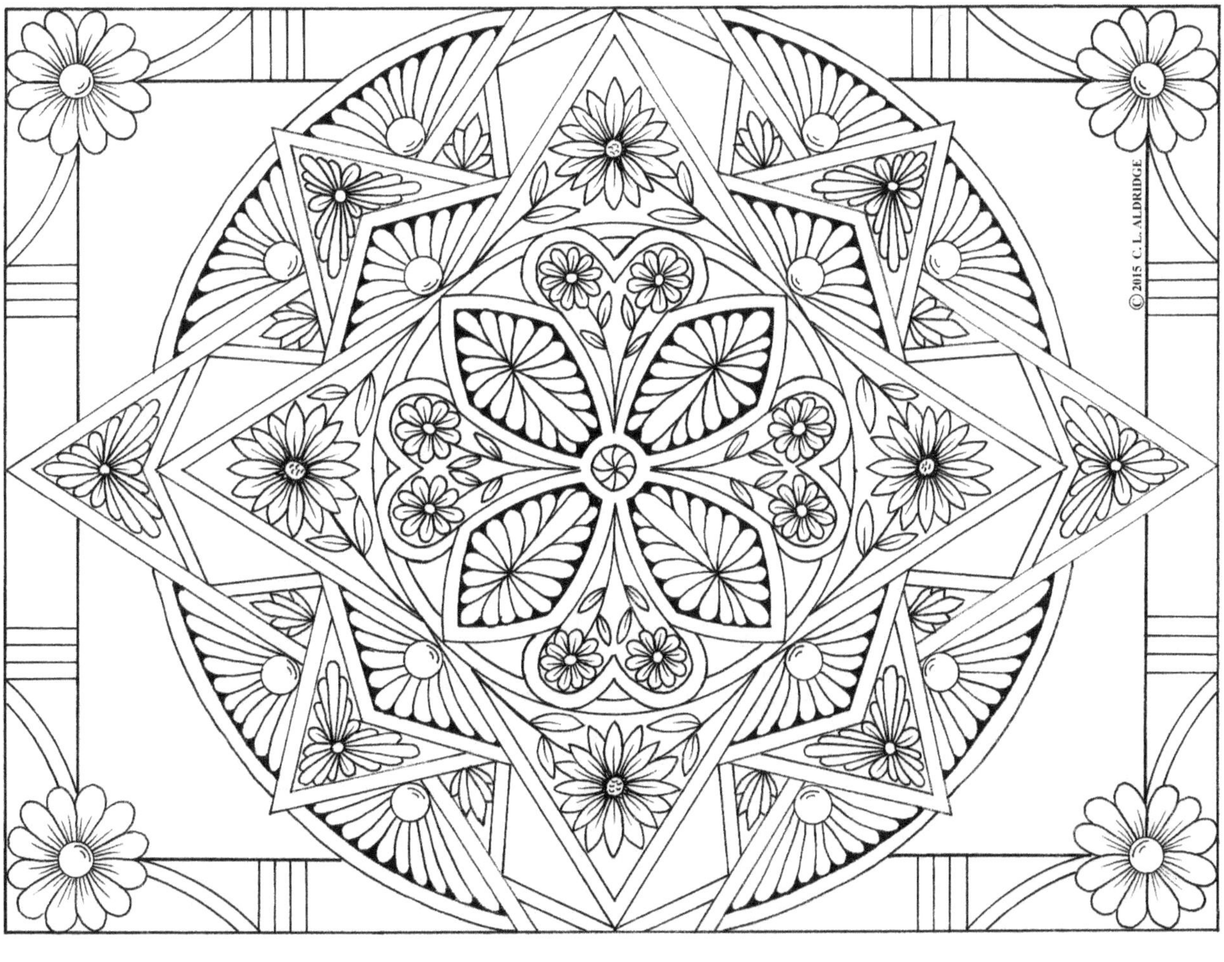
© 2015 C. L. ALDRIDGE

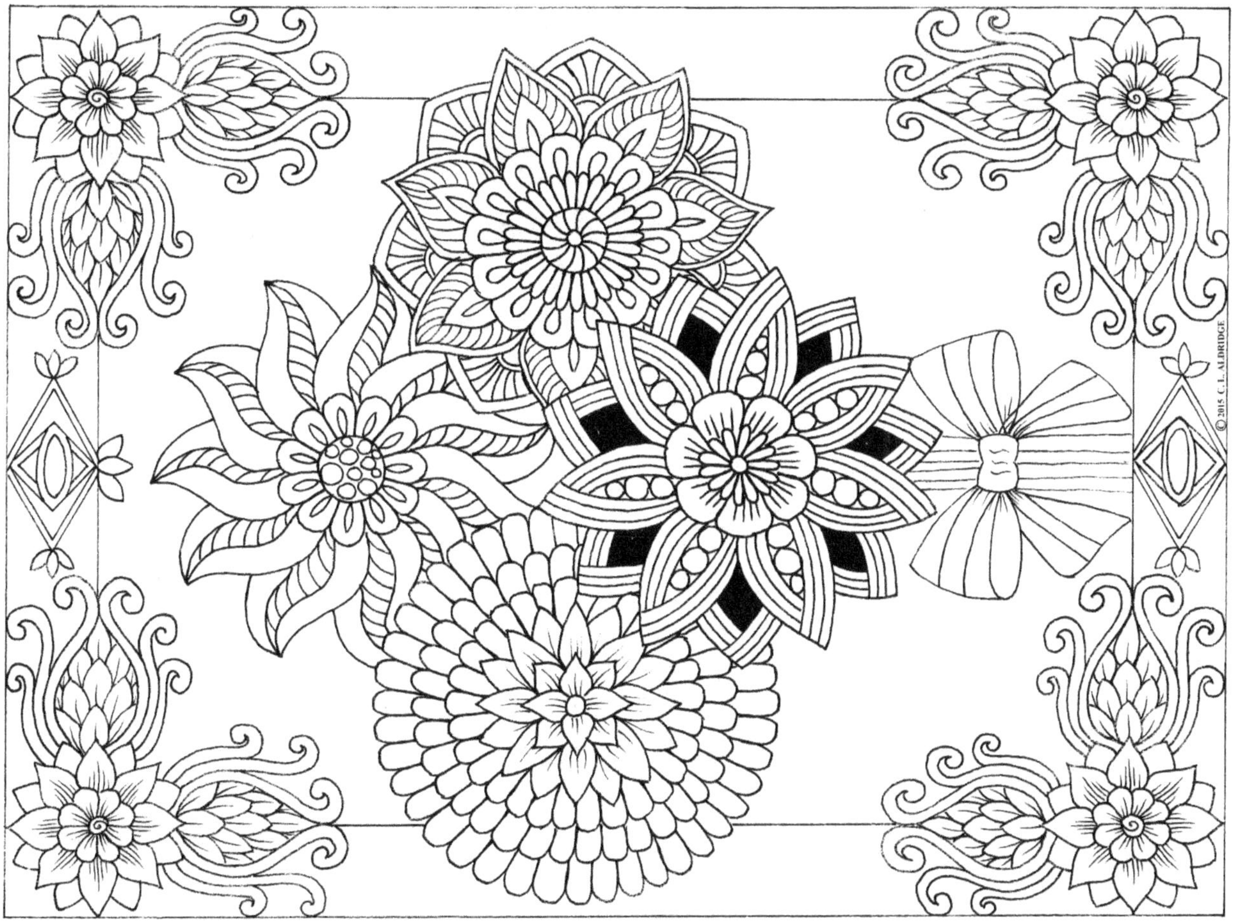
© 2015 C. L. ALDRIDGE

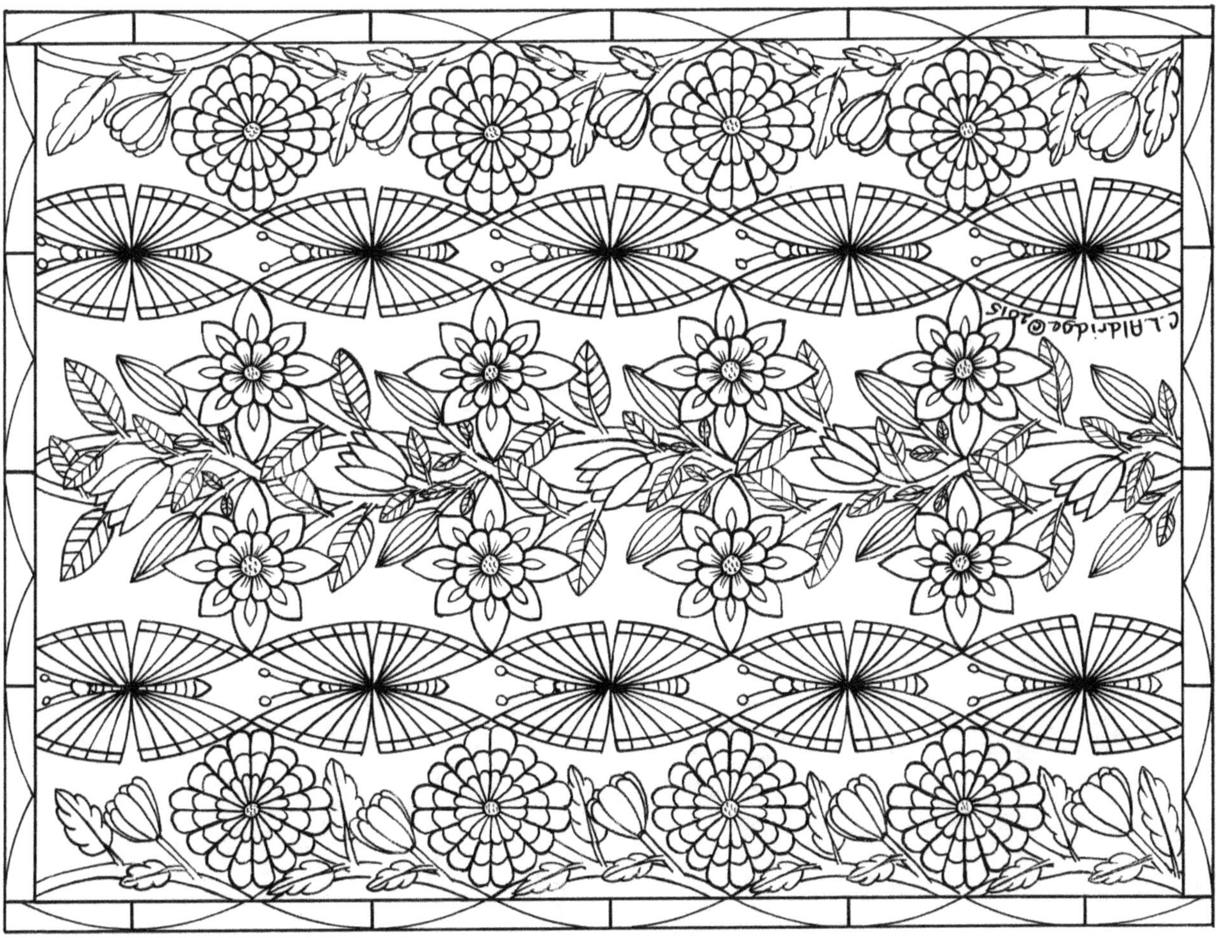
C.L.Aldridge©2015

©2016 C.L. Aldridge

This page has intentionally been left blank for use as either a blotting page or color testing page.

This page has intentionally been left blank for use as either a blotting page or color testing page.

This page has intentionally been left blank for use as either
a blotting page or color testing page.